The Secret of Greatness

Destined to Succeed and to Be Great

Daniel Nana Kwame Opare

The Secret of Greatness
Copyright © 2015 by **Daniel Nana Kwame Opare**. All rights reserved.

No part of this publication may be reproduced, stored in a retrieval system or transmitted in any way by any means, electronic, mechanical, photocopy, recording or otherwise, without the prior permission of the author except as provided by USA copyright law.

All characters appearing in this work are fictitious. Any resemblance to real persons, living or dead, is purely coincidental.

The opinions expressed by the author are not necessarily those of Revival Waves of Glory Books & Publishing.

Published by Revival Waves of Glory Books & Publishing
PO Box 596| Litchfield, Illinois 62056 USA
www.revivalwavesofgloryministries.com

Revival Waves of Glory Books & Publishing is committed to excellence in the publishing industry.

Book design copyright © 2015 by Revival Waves of Glory Books & Publishing. All rights reserved.

EBook: 978-1-329-07149-0
Paperback: 978-1-329-07145-2
Hardcover: 978-1-329-07147-6

Published in the United States of America

TABLE OF CONTENTS

Preface 5

Acknowledgment 6

Dedication 7

Chapter One DESTINED TO SUCCEED AND TO BE GREAT THROUGH ACCOMPLISHMENT OF DIVINE PURPOSE 8

Chapter Two THE POWER OF THE MIND 25

Chapter Three THE POWER OF CHANGE 33

Chapter four THE SECRET OF AFRICA'S UNDERDEVELOPMENT AND THE WAY OUT TO GREATNESS 43

About the Author 56

Preface

Many people suffer in life just because they don't know who they are and what they are destined for. This book will help you to know who you are and what you are destined for in order to break through in life.

Many people also fail in life due to their negative response to change. Change is permanent, constant and so powerful that it affects everything under the sun.

With the exception of God, everything goes through change.

Since everything changes, one's success or failure in life depends largely on his or her reaction or response to change. For this reason, this book has been written to draw believers' attention to the power of change in order to help them make it in life.

This book will also enable you to know the reason why Africa is underdeveloped despite its numerous natural resources.

The Bible says, "For lack of knowledge my people are destroyed". This book is full of divine truth. Read it to transform your life.

All the quotations in this book are taken from the Gideon international version of the Bible.

Acknowledgment

I thank God, the owner of the universe for bestowing upon me wisdom and insight to write this book.

I also thank Mr. Ashong and Mrs. The director of shepherd printing press for his immerse contribution to the success of this book.

May the Lord bless him according to his riches in Christ Jesus.

Dedication

To: Deaconess Faustina Mensah, Deaconess LindaTeye, Madam Margaret Tiwaa alias Sister Yaw and all my mothers in Christ.

Author

Daniel N. K. Opare

e-mail:roselmaclean@yahoo.com

danielkwame481@yahoo.com

nagasnagasty@aol.com

Tel: +233-269851768

+233(0)209938929

Chapter One
DESTINED TO SUCCEED AND TO BE GREAT THROUGH ACCOMPLISHMENT OF DIVINE PURPOSE

God created the planet earth and handed everything on it to human beings to control; hence, nobody was born by accident. We all came into this world by God for a purpose-to control, to rule, to till and to enjoy the fruits of the earth, but the living standard of many people makes it look as if some people came to escort others. The truth is, nobody came to escort anyone; neither did anyone come by accident.

All of us came into this world with unique qualities to control, to till, and to enjoy the fruits of the earth: but due to ignorance, many people are living below the standard.

None of us was born to suffer or to be inferior to others. We were all created in the image and likeness of God to accomplish His purpose on earth. It is written, "And God said, Let us make man in our image, after our likeness, and let them have dominion over the fish of the sea and over the fowl of the air, and over the cattle, and over all the earth, and over every creeping thing that creepeth upon the earth. So God created man in his own image, in the image of God created he him; male and female created he them". (Genesis 1:26 -27)

The statement: God created man (Male and Female) in His own image and likeness implies that, God created human beings and endowed us with his own wisdom, Moral characteristics, abilities and potentials to have dominion over everything on the earth.

So, according to the above scripture, human beings posses the abilities to create, rule, and to change conditions and situations. It is written, "In the beginning God created the Heaven and the earth.

And the earth was without form, and void; and darkness was upon the face of the deep. And God said, let there be light and there was light". (Genesis 1:1-3) God is a creator, a ruler, a changer of situations and conditions and above all, full of wisdom and so has he made human beings.

All of us possess the wisdom and the abilities of God to create, to invent, to rule, and to change situations: therefore, do not allow yourself to be overcome by situations and conditions.

You are greater than poverty just because you are the ruler of the earth and everything therein. So therefore, change your mind from inferiority complex and all kinds of negative thoughts; arise, and glorify God by demonstrating his abilities, potentials and gifts lying dormant in you and your life will be transformed no matter your geographical location.

In fact, when a person is born into an advanced country or a rich family, his or her success becomes easier:

But know that, the advanced country or the rich families were not made by nature, but by human beings like you; therefore, never allow yourself to be overcome by anything, be it the country or the family in which you were born; for nothing on this earth can stop or prevent you from becoming successful except you yourself; therefore, arise and build a wealthy family tomorrow from today through the talents, abilities, potentials and the gifts in you.

The decision and action you take today will determine the state and condition of your life tomorrow.

Note, wherever you find yourself in this world, it is not by accident. It is God who determines a person's locality. It is written, "God that made the world and all things therein, seeing that he is Lord of heaven and earth dwelled not in temples made with men's hands, as though he needed anything, seeing he gives to all life, breath and all things

And hath made of one blood (man) all nations of men for to dwell on all the face of the earth, and has determined the time before appointed and the bounds of their habitation". (Acts17:24- 26) So therefore, whatever family, tribe, country or continent in which you find yourself, it was God who put you there; and it was for a purpose-to save, restore, transform, build and to change conditions and situations.

When David was anointed by Samuel to be king of Israel, the Spirit of God departed from Saul, and came to rest upon David; and an evil spirit was commanded by God to harass Saul.

Because of that, Saul was asked by his servants to find him a man who knows how to play the harp very well, so that when he plays, he would be refreshed from his depression, stress, etc. by the evil spirit.

And since David was very skillful in playing the harp, he was brought to Saul in the palace and never went back to his Father's house again. Then, it came to pass; there was a war between Israel and Philistine (Palestine); Saul left David in the palace and went with the army to fight the Philistines.

When Saul left home to fight the Philistines, David, a man who had developed a strong love for sheep rearing, came back home from the palace to take care of his father's Sheep.

Jesse, the Father of David, had eight sons. Three of them were soldiers; hence, they were with Saul in the battle field.

The rest, with the exception of David were with their father at home, yet Jesse did not send any of them to deliver food to his brothers in the battlefield: but when David arrived home from the palace, he was sent to do so.

Jesse, having waited till David came back home from the palace before sending him to deliver food to his brothers in the battle field does not mean the rest of his sons who were with him in the house were stubborn; neither does it mean anything negative as one may think of; but rather, for a divine purpose.

God sent David, a young man upon whom the Spirit of God had rested through the anointing of Samuel the prophet, to the battlefield through Jesse his father to deliver

Israel from the hands of the Philistines by killing Goliath. And David himself, having known this, said unto his elder brother; "Is it not a cause?" When he became angry with him for coming to the battlefield. (1Samuel 16:13-22, 17:1-51)

David found himself in the battlefield purposely for the salvation of Israel from the hands of the Philistines. Therefore, whatever family, tribe, or Country in which you find yourself, God put you there for a purpose – to restore, to save, to transform and to change situations and conditions.

Note, you are not here on earth, neither in the family nor in the country in which you were born by your own will. It was God who brought you and put you there to accomplish his own purpose.

As a person who is assigned to accomplish a task is given everything needed for the task, so has God provided you with all the equipment such as gifts, abilities, potentials and talents to accomplish the purpose; so therefore, discover it, accomplish it, and your life will be transformed.

Discover the purpose and pursue it with a great vision

The purpose is determined by the abilities, potentials, talents and the gifts in you. The abilities, Potentials, talents and the gifts show the kind of work God has assigned to each and everyone on this earth.

Nobody could easily succeed in a genuine manner; neither be famous nor be remembered even after death without it.

One's talents, gifts, potentials or abilities could be meant for sports, theater, art, selling, farming, inventions, innovations, etc. The abilities, potentials, talents and the gifts in you are unlimited sources of wealth; they are full of money. They are the means by which God has destined each and everyone to succeed in life.

King Solomon became the most famous and richest man in his generation. It was his gift of wisdom that made him the richest man in his era. The Book of books, says that, "All the kings of the earth sought the presence of Solomon with gold, silver, horses, mules, spices, raiment, and harness to hear his wisdom". (2 Chronicles 9:22-24)

Joseph was made the prime minister of Egypt, the land of his slavery by Pharaoh. It was his gift and ability of interpretation of a dream that caused him to become the prime minister. (Genesis 41:1-42)

Daniel also was made the governor of the whole province (state) of Babylon by Nebuchadnezzar. It was his gift and ability of interpretation of a dream that caused him to become the governor. (Daniel 2:46-48)

The above mentioned personalities became great by using their abilities, and gifts to the benefits of others. This obviously indicates that, service is the means by which a person becomes great in life.

Hence, Jesus Christ, the greatest man ever lived, said, "Whoever desires to be great, let him minister (serve)". Matthew 20:26, Mark 10:43)

The service used here is not a matter of being a maid, no, but rather, using the abilities, potentials, talents, gifts, wealth, power, position, as well as whatever in hands to the benefits and happiness of others. It is the only means by which a person is regarded as great in society, nation and the world as a whole.

Example, Wilbur and Ovule wrights, Alexander Graham Bell, Bill Gates and the rest, became great through service by using their abilities, potentials, talents and the gifts to invent aircraft, telephone, etc., for the benefits and happiness of others.

So Therefore, discover the abilities, potentials, talents and the gifts in you, which determine your task on earth: and after the discovery, never joke with it, pursue it with a great vision and use it to the benefits and happiness of others, and your life will be transformed. You will also be great.

The abilities, potentials, talents and the gifts which determine a person's work on earth, is discovered by what one can do best as well as what is termed as a hobby.

David, the youngest among the eight sons of Jesse developed a very strong love for sheep rearing, in the sense that he even fought with the lion and bear to deliver the sheep from their mouth.

And this love for sheep rearing seemed to him as a hobby, but in actual fact God was using it to prepare him for his assignment on earth.

David was destined by God to rule Israel; hence, his strong love for sheep rearing was an act of God to prepare him for his kingship task.

I also developed a very strong love for Bible reading and it seemed to me as a hobby; meanwhile I have been destined to impart divine knowledge. For this reason, never joke with your hobby as well as what you can do better.

The abilities, potentials, talents and the gifts which determine a person's assignment or work on earth can also be discovered through prayer, dream, vision, prophecy and inner feeling, as well as hearing of the voice of God.

After the discovery, appreciate it, love it, cherish it, honor it, sharpen it, and pursue it with a great vision. The sharpen can be through seminar, formal, distant, informal, or self education. It is the only way a person can excel in his or her field of ability.

Many footballers in the world are naturally gifted but those of them who embark on extra training always excel than those who do not. Therefore, after the discovery of the abilities, potentials, gifts and the talents, sharpen them in order to excel in life.

Note, in the pursuit of the vision, be very careful about the people around you, especially those who do not respect your vision, talents, gifts and potentials: if possible do away with them.

There are three types of people in the world. These are: helpers, parasites and destroyers. The helpers are people who help others to achieve their visions in the form of exhortation, motivation, capital, etc.

The parasites are people who are only interested in enjoying the blessings of other people.

The destroyers are people who destroy visions of other people in the form of discouragement, sabotage, etc.

Unfortunately, the helpers are very few in the world, especially in Africa. So be very careful about the people you share your ideas and visions with; lest you regret at the end. It is written "Give not that which is holy unto the dogs, neither cast your pearls before swine, lest they trample them under their feet, and turn again and rend you". (Matthew 7:6)

The pearls and the holy things are the things you value such as ideas, vision, properties, etc. Do not lay them before or hand them over or disclose them to people who do not value them, lest they destroy them in the form of discouragement, mismanagement, etc. and turn to mock you at the end.

A certain woman, a wife of one of the late junior prophets, said unto Elisha; the then prophet of the Nation: "Thy servant my husband is dead; and thou knowest that thy servant did fear the Lord: and the creditor is come to take unto him my two sons to be bondmen. And Elisha said unto her; tell me, what hast thou in the house?

And she said, Thine handmaid hath not anything in the house, save a pot of oil. Then Elisha said unto her, Go, borrow thee vessels abroad of all thy neighbors, even empty vessels; borrow not a few. And when thou art come in, thou shalt shut the door upon thee, and upon thy sons, and shalt pour out the oil into all those vessels and thou shalt set aside that which is full.

So she went from him, and shut the door upon her and upon her sons, who brought the vessels to her; and she poured out. And it came to pass, when the vessels were full, that she said unto her son, Bring me yet a vessel. And he said unto her, there is not a vessel more. And the oil stayed". (2kings 4:1-6)

Why did Elisha tell the woman to pour out the little oil into the vessels in her room? Elisha told the woman to do so because of discouragement of men (both sexes.) In fact, if the woman was to fill the several vessels with the one little pot of oil in the open house, people would use all kinds of words to discourage her from filling the vessels with the little oil.

Again, God said unto Abraham, "Take now thy son, thine only son Isaac, whom thou lovest; and offer him for a burnt offering unto me".

Abraham therefore obeyed God and made the attempt to honor the voice of God without the knowledge of Salah his wife and the servants. And because of what he did, God said unto him, "By myself have I sworn, said the LORD, for because thou hast done this thing, and hast not withheld thy son, thine only son.

That in blessing I will bless thee, and in multiplying I will multiply thy seed as the star of the heaven, and as the sand which is upon the sea shore; and thy seed shall possess the gate of his enemies; and in thy seed shall all the nations of the earth be blessed; because thou hast obeyed my voice". (Genesis 22: 1-18)

If Abraham had revealed to Salah, his wife and the servants what God told him to do; they would have discouraged him from making the attempt to sacrifice Isaac his son to God. For this reason, in the pursuit of the vision; be very cautious about the people around you: but rather, let God be in the center of it, for without him you cannot make it.

You cannot make it without God

It is written, "Without me, you can do nothing". (John 15:5) As the plants sprout out of the earth and remain in it in order to bear fruit, so can no one succeed in a genuine manner without the one who created him or her.

God said unto Zerubabel: "Not by might, nor by power, but by my Spirit, said the Lord of hosts". (Zechariah 4:6) God commanded Cyrus the king of Persia, the then king of the world to allow his temple in Jerusalem-Judah, which was demolished by Nebuchadnezzar to be re-built by his people, the Israelites. (Ezra 1:1-3)

For this reason, the king made Zerubabel the governor of Judah, and commanded him to build the temple. (Haggai 2:1-4)

However, Zerubbabel, being made the governor of Judah with the authority of the king of the world to build the temple, thought he could easily build it irrespective of the harassment from the surrounding nations. But God said unto him; indeed, you are the governor of Judah with the authority from the emperor to build the temple, yet you cannot overcome the enemies who have risen against the building of the temple to be able to build it without me: Hence, the statement, not by might nor by power, but by my Spirit".

So therefore, let God take the center stage in your vision through prayer, for without him you cannot make it irrespective of your abilities, talents, potentials, Skills, experience, knowledge, etc. Talk to God always in prayer and he will give you directions through vision, prophecy, dreams, inner feeling, voice or the scriptures. Act upon them and you will make it in life.

David, the most successful and famous king in Israel, fought throughout his lifetime with the surrounding nations and beyond and conquered all of them. David was able to conquer all the surrounding nations just because in spite of the Spirit of God upon him through the anointing of Samuel, he allowed himself to be guided by the instructions, directions and the word of God. David never went to war without enquiring from God. (1 Samuel 30: 1-8, 2 Samuel 5:17-19)

He allowed the word of God to be a lamp unto his feet and a light unto his path; and because of that, he never lost any battle in his life. For this reason, in the pursuit of the vision, do not take God out of it, talk to him always in prayer, and let his word guide you and you will make it.

People who take God out of their visions, tasks, etc. and move in their own direction; normally bring many problems upon their families, tribes, nations and themselves as well. It is written, "Now when Jesus was born in Bethlehem of Judea in the days of Herod the king, behold, there came wise men from the east to Jerusalem, saying, where is he that is born king of the Jews? For we have seen his star in the east, and are come to worship him.

When Herod the king had heard these things, he was troubled, and all Jerusalem with him. And when he had gathered all the chief priests and scribes of the people together, he demanded of them where Christ should be born.

And they said unto him, in Bethlehem of Judea: for thus it is written by the prophets. Then Herod, when he had privily called the wise men, inquired of them diligently what time the star appeared and he sent them to Bethlehem, and Said, Go and search diligently for the young child; and when ye have found him, bring me word again, that I may come and worship him also. When they had heard the king, they departed; and, lo, the star, which they saw in the east, went before them, till it came and stood over where the young child was.

And when they were come into the house, they saw the young child with Mary his mother, and fell down, and worshipped him: and when they had opened their treasures, they presented unto him gifts, gold, and frankincense, and myrrh. And being warned of God in a dream that they should not return to Herod, they departed into their own country another way.

And when they were departed, behold, the angel of the Lord appeareth to Joseph, saying, Arise, and take the young child and his mother, and flee into Egypt, and be thou there until I bring thee word: for Herod will seek the young child to destroy him.

When he arose, he took the young child and his mother by night, and departed into Egypt: Then Herod, when he saw that he was mocked of the wise men, was exceeding wroth, and sent forth, and slew all the children that were in Bethlehem, and in all the coasts thereof from two years old and under, according to the time which he had diligently inquired of the wise men". (Matthew 2:1-16)

However, the men were called "Wise men" just because they feared God. The Bible says, "The fear of the Lord is the begging of wisdom." (Psalm 111:10)

The men were Gentiles, yet they feared God. And not only did they fear God; they were also waiting for the appearing of the messiah.

Note, the coming of the messiah was mentioned right from the first generation (Genesis 3:15); hence, it was known to many nations.

So when Jesus Christ, the messiah of the world was born, God revealed it to the wise men who were waiting for it, and directed them to where he was born through a star. These men followed the direction of the star to Israel.

But unfortunately, when they reached Israel, they ignored the direction of the star, and moved in their own direction with the mentality that every king is born in a royal family. So they ignored the direction of the star and moved with their own thinking to the palace.

And because of what they did, God allowed the children to be killed by Herod to tell us that whoever ignores divine direction, and does his or her own thing, end up by getting him or herself into a lot of problems. It is written, "There is a way that seems right unto a man, but the end thereof are the ways of death". (Proverbs 16:25)

For this reason, irrespective of your abilities, talents, potentials, knowledge, experience, etc. in the pursuit of the vision, do not ignore the directions and the instructions of God; but rather, act upon them and the desires of your heart shall be established. It is written, "Commit thy works unto the Lord, and thy thoughts shall be established". (Proverbs 16:3)

Problem

Nevertheless, in the pursuit of the vision, problems and challenges will come or arise from all angles, both physical and spiritual; but know that success or glory is not gained on silver platter, therefore, don't throw in the towel.

People from all angles, both Christians and non Christians, as well as relatives, friends, and even parents will do or say all kinds of things in the form of insult, disdain, etc. to discourage you, yet don't give up.

Note the life, ways and actions of a person with great vision are abnormal and stupid in the sight of ordinary people; so therefore, do not let their words and actions discourage you: for you alone know what God has destined you for or what you have heard or seen. It is written, "The kingdom of heaven is like unto treasure hid in a field; which when a man hath found, he hideth, and selleth all that he hath, and buyeth that field." It is also written, "The kingdom of God is like unto a merchant man, seeking goodly pearls: who, when he had found one pearl of great price, went and sold all that he had, and bought it". (Matthew 13:44-46)

The above parables are one in meaning, both spiritual and physical; which indicate that, glory or success is not free; there is a price for it. As a person has to do away with things he or she delights in most but are contradictory to the word of God, in order to gain heaven, so is there a price for glory or success.

The men sold all their properties, everything they had, and bought the field and the pearl respectively. The actions of these two men of great visions would seem abnormal and stupid in the sight of people who did not know the precious things in the field as well as the pearl.

So know that in the pursuit of the vision, the price of success or glory will make your life, ways and actions look abnormal and stupid in the sight of ordinary people and because of that they will insult you, yet don't give up; for you alone know what God has destined you for or what you have heard or seen.

David was rebuked by his elder brother for coming to the battlefield; but because he knew why he was brought there, he was not discouraged by his brother's insult; he went on to accomplish it by killing Goliath to save Israel from the hands of the Philistines: and this made him the most popular man in Israel.

Therefore, in the pursuit of the vision, do not be discouraged of problems and discouragements, nor be frightened by yesterday's failure, but rather, learn from it, stand firm, be focus, let excuse, laziness, procrastination, fear of failure and extravagance be out of your life: associate yourself with people; God fearing ones whose contributions could help lift you to the height: and let prayer, love, truth, righteousness, faithfulness, charity, humility, patience, obedience, discipline, perseverance, confidence and excellence be your hall mark: and you will make it in life.

Finally, do not choose a career nor enter into business, occupation or profession which does not fall within your abilities, potentials, talents and gifts.

Parents, especially those of you in Africa, discover the subjects your children like best and let them pursue and they will make it in life.

Heads of states, especially those of you in Africa, draw your economic policies and educational structures to accommodate every ability, talent, potential and gift for growth, development, and the betterment of the individuals and the Countries as well.

Chapter Two
THE POWER OF THE MIND

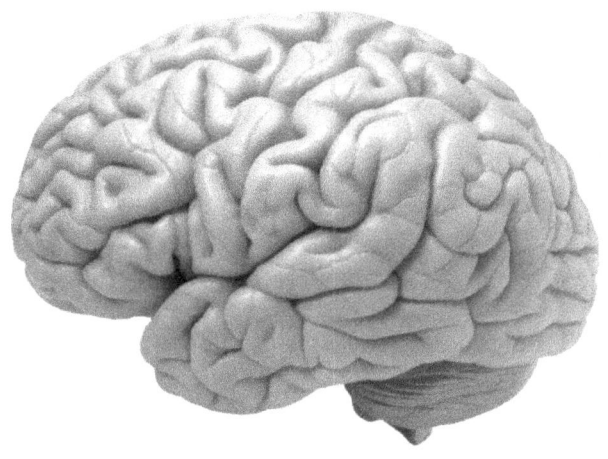

The human brain

God created human beings and endowed us with his own wisdom to control and to enjoy the goodness of the earth, but unfortunately, many people struggle in life due to their inability to cause the mind to demonstrate its awesome abilities.

The mind is full of divine wisdom and ability for creativity and transformation; hence, the ability of the mind is marvelous.

Things like electricity, aircraft, television, telephone and the like which are products of the mind, show how powerful the mind is.

The mind is the human consciousness that originates and manifests in the form of imagination, thought and perception in the organ called brain; that controls movement, memory, thoughts and feeling of the body.

The mind which is the human consciousness that originates in the brain is the steering wheel as well as the inner eye of the body. It is the determinant of a person's outcome in life; hence, it is the source of wealth, success, riches as well as failure. Whatever direction the mind is channeled to, so shall the result be. It is written, "As a man thinketh in his heart, so is he."(Proverbs 3: 7).

The mind controls the total well-being of the body, so it serves as the battled field.

When it is captured, possessed, or controlled, by an evil force or wrong information; so shall the life, attitude and the manifestation of the body be.

Note, success comes from the inner being, and the eye that lightings the inner being to come out with the success is the mind. Hence, when it is affected, the whole body becomes good for nothing. It is written, "The light of the body is the eye. If, therefore thine eye be single, thy whole body shall be full of light. But if thine eye be evil, thy whole body shall be full of darkness.

If, therefore the light that is in thee be darkness, how great is that darkness." (Matthew 6:22-23)

The mind is a person's greatest God-given equipment for transformation; hence, it is the source of development in life, society and a nation as a whole.

Note, because it is the mind that controls and determines the total well being of a person, when a woman is in labor, it is the head of the child, which is the seat of the mind that directs the entire body by coming out first to make the labor possible and easy. For this reason, it is difficult for a person to succeed in life without the demonstration of the mind.

The mind is the warehouse and faculty of success. All the man-made or creation of man such as cars, planes, machines, etc., came into being through the application of the mind. Therefore, transform your life through the application of the mind in the form of deep positive imagination and creative thinking. All ideals, visions, discoveries, creating, etc. are conceived in the mind before it materializes in the open.

The seeing ability of the mind is far beyond the external eye of the body; hence, possibilities and success are always seen with the mind.

The mind is so powerful that with it the impossibility is possible. It doesn't matter how small your thinking engine may be, you can do exploits. Therefore, arise, change your mind from inferiority complex and all kinds of negative thoughts, and transform your life through deep positive thinking; for all the inventors, innovators, discoverers as well as men and women of achievements in the world like Bill Gates the inventor of Microsoft,

Wilbur and Ovule Wright the inventors of aircraft, Sir Isaac Newton the discoverer of the law of gravity and the inventor of calculus, Albert Einstein the developer of relativity and a key player in the invention of atomic energy, Alexander Graham Bell the inventor of telephone, etc., became achievers through deep positive imagination and thoughts.

Note, it doesn't necessarily mean one has to be a PHD holder before being able to think deeply about things. No, even though it is an added advantage. So therefore, do not be mediocre, naive and myopic; think deeply about things before you take decision, action, or believe anything; neither, be hesitant to ask questions, and by so doing, it will be well with you in the sense that you will avoid unpleasant surprises in the form of fatal mistakes.

FEED THE MIND

Since the mind is the determinant of a person's outcome in life, it causes the body to struggle in life if is not fed. This is another cardinal reason why many people struggle in life. Therefore let the mind be fed first, and when it is satisfied it will provide the needs of the body without struggling.

However, to feed the mind is to acquire knowledge. Knowledge is the food as well as the fuel of the mind. Knowledge also serves as the platform of the mind for greatness.

According to the Oxford advance learner's dictionary, knowledge is the information, understanding and skills that a person gain through education or experience. It is difficult to succeed without knowledge. It is written, "My people are destroyed for lack of knowledge" (Hosea 4:6) it is also written, "My people are gone into captivity because they have no knowledge". (Isaiah 5:13)

Knowledge brings glory, success, growth, progress and development in life, society and a nation as a whole. It is written, "And by knowledge shall the chambers be filled with riches."(Proverbs 24:4)

Knowledge is a key to success in every sphere of life; hence, a country with a high rate of people with low level of knowledge suffers from under-development. Without knowledge, irrespective of your gifts, talents, potential or abilities you will find it difficult in life; therefore, acquire knowledge.

Paul, undoubtedly the most outstanding man of God in history was blessed with all the five accession gifts of Jesus Christ, namely Apostle, Prophet, Teacher, Pastor and evangelist as well as almost all the nine gifts of the Holy Spirit, namely, the word of wisdom, the word of knowledge, Faith, healing, Miracles, prophecy, discerning of spirits, divers kinds of tongues and interpretation of tongues spelled out in Ephesians 4:11 and 1Corinthians 12:8-10 respectively, yet he continued to seek knowledge.

He said unto Timothy "The cloak that I left at Troas with Carpus, when thou comest, bring with thee and the books." (2 Timothy 4:13)

Paul continued to acquire knowledge and because of that, he excelled in the ministry than all his peers.

Daniel, one of the great prophets in history, was a man full of wisdom, revelation and insight, yet he continued to acquire knowledge. It is written, "In the first year of Darius the son of Ahasuerus, of the seed of the Medes, which was made king over the realm of the Chaldeans, I Daniel understood by books the number of the years, whereof the word of the Lord came to Jeremiah the prophet, that he would accomplish seventy years in the desolations of Jerusalem. And I set my face unto the Lord God, to seek by prayer and supplications, with fasting, and sackcloth, and ashes." (Daniel 9:1-3)

If Daniel had not continued to seek knowledge he wouldn't have known the set time for the restoration to intercede for its accomplishment.

So therefore, lack of knowledge could be described as blindness. This is the reason why people with low level of knowledge are normally taken for granted in many countries especially in Africa. Therefore, seek knowledge.

Reduce the expenses on the stomach as well as the body and feed the mind with knowledge and it will be well with you.

SOURCES OF KNOWLEDGE

However, apart from the formal system of acquiring knowledge which is through the educational institutions, knowledge is also acquired through self-education. This is done through reading.

All knowledge and wisdom are hidden in books, both the divine and the secular; hence, the books are a rich source of knowledge and wisdom. But unfortunately, many people don't like reading.

Note: Life transforming knowledge is not normally taught in the academia or the educational institutions; therefore, read books. Countries whose citizens are not interested in reading, develop at a very slow pace.

Another source of knowledge and wisdom is nature. Nature is a rich source of knowledge and wisdom. It is written, "Go to the ant, thou sluggard; consider his ways and be wise." (Proverbs 6:6)

Nature is full of wisdom and knowledge; hence, things like aircraft, ship, sub-marine and computer were all invented through the study of birds, ducks, fish and the human mind respectively.

Knowledge and wisdom can also be acquired through seminars, sermon and the media, which are: television, radio, internet and newspapers. Therefore, do not listen, read or watch them only for the sake of entertainment and current affairs but also as sources of wisdom and knowledge.

Note, just as precious and valuable natural resources like gold, oil, and the like are not found on the surface of the earth, so is success also not gained on silver platter. So therefore, it is difficult for a person to succeed in a genuine manner without launching out into the deep.

Jesus said unto Peter, "Launch into the deep for a catch". Peter therefore inclined his ears onto the voice of Jesus and launched into the deep. And when he did that, he caught a great number of fish. (Luke 5:1-6)

For this reason, do not be narrow-minded, but rather, dive into the deep through information, knowledge, imagination and thought.

Be abreast with information always on whatever work you are doing and let it serve as a platform for the mind because the mind is the faculty of development and success as well as the total wellbeing of the body.

The ability of the mind is awesome. Therefore, do not inferior yourself, but rather, broaden your mind with knowledge which is the platform of the mind for greatness, and let God be your anchor and it will be well with you.

Chapter Three
THE POWER OF CHANGE

Many companies have collapsed, many people have lost their jobs, many people have lost their positions, many people are living below the standard of living due to their negative response to change. Change is permanent and constant.

Everything under heaven goes through change. There is nothing on earth which does not change. Everything on this earth is affected by change. Change is not a respecter of condition, person, race, stature, language, etc. it affects everything. Change is so constant and powerful that, nobody can stop its occurrence.

The problem can only be solved if its source is destroyed, erased, or controlled. But unfortunately, with regard to change its source or the force behind it cannot be destroyed by anyone.

Example: the sun is the force behind day and night. Who can destroy it to stop the occurrence of day and night? It is written, "And God said, Let there be lights in the firmament of the heaven to divide the day from the night; and let them be for signs, and for seasons, and for days, and years". (Genesis 1:14)

God created the universe and everything in it and set up forces, laws, rules and principles to control them; and change is no exception. God has made this known unto us by saying unto Job, and the Israelites through Jeremiah respectively: "Knowest thou the ordinances of heaven? Canst thou set the dominion thereof in the earth? Have I not appointed the ordinances of heaven and earth?" (Job 38:33, Jeremiah 33:25)

So, since change is also caused by divine established forces, laws, rules and principles which some scientists after discovering they claim them to be theirs, day and night, summer and winter, spring and autumn, rain season and dry season, gray hair and wrinkles, etc. will continue to occur; we cannot stop them. It is written, "While the earth remaineth, seed-time and harvest, and cold and heat, and summer and winter, and day and night shall not cease". (Genesis 8:22)

However, there are two main types of change. These are: natural change, and artificial or scientific change.

Out of the natural change, there are two types of them. These are: Physical change and biological change.

So in all, there are three types of change which are: physical change, biological change and artificial or scientific change.

The Physical change: the physical change is a change that happens around us such as day and night, summer and winter, rain season and dry season, etc.

The Biological change: the biological change is a change that happens to us such as wrinkles, gray hair, etc.

The Artificial or scientific change: the artificial or scientific change is a change that happens through us such as inventions, innovations, etc.

All these three types of change are caused by divine established forces, rules, laws and principles.

Note, God created human beings and endowed us with wisdom, abilities, talents and potentials to have dominion over everything on earth. So it is the divine wisdom, potentials and the abilities in us that act as a force behind the artificial or the scientific change: hence, all the three types of change are caused by divine established forces, rules, laws and principles.

So whether you like it or not, change will continue to occur; nobody can stop it. For this reason, do not oppose change, but rather, respond to it positively.

Note, success and failure depend largely on the reaction or responds to change: therefore, whoever refuses to plan for, or respond positively to change, does it at his or her detriment.

Note, God does not do anything without a purpose. Since change is caused by divine established forces, laws, rules, and principles, it is of God. And since it is of God, it is for a purpose; a purpose for our own good.

For instance, if any of these: day, night, rain season, dry season, summer, and winter should continuously occur forever without the occurrence of its opposite event, what would be the outcome?

And since the outcome would not be good for lives or living things, God established change to prevent the disaster. So, God established change for a purpose; a purpose for our own good.

Example: Night occurs to cause us to sleep in order for the body to regain its strength. Whoever refuses to comply with it will either grow lean or fall sick. As night occurs for us to sleep in order for the body to regain its strength, so does day also occur for us to work for a livelihood.

Jesus said; "I must work while it is day." Whoever refuses to work during the day will automatically end up in poverty. For this reason, never joke with change to jeopardize your life.

Example, what would the state and conditions of the farms in the savannah belt or zone whose owners will not embark on irrigation to manage them but rather oppose dry season be?

What would the state and conditions of people in the temperate and the Polar Regions who will not embark on the use of heater and the other means of heat to warm themselves but rather oppose winter be?

What would the state and conditions of companies and organizations which will not embark on the use of a computer but rather oppose it be?

Change is so powerful that, no matter your race, geographical location, educational background, skill, experience, qualities, financial status, etc. It will affect you: therefore, do not oppose it; but rather, act like the men of Issachar: smells it, sense it, foresee it, understand it, plan and respond to it positively in order to survive, to maintain, and to meet the current and future market demands and employment requirements.

The Bible says that, "The children of Issachar were men that had understanding of the times, to know what Israel ought to do". (1 chronicles 12:33)

People who do not oppose change, but rather plan for or respond positively to it, always make it in life.

Types of people in the world in terms of response to change

However, with regard to response or reaction to change, there are three types of people in the world. These are: planers, boasters and detractors.

Planners; the planners are people who see change as a principle of creation, as well as a part of human life; hence, they prepare for it, plan for it, adjust to it, submit to it, etc. They respond positively to change and because of that, they always make headway in life.

Companies and organizations whose leaders are within this group of people never collapse; they always stand tall. Example: there are certain football clubs in Europe. Years ago, these clubs were not regarded as football giants in the world.

However, they quickly accepted the changing trends in football and adopted measures to meet them; and because of that, today, they have also emerged as giants in the world club football. And one of these clubs is Chelsea.

Boasters: the boasters are people who never do anything positive in times of change. They always live on their past glory. Instead of responding positively to change in order to make headway, they rather boast themselves of their past glory or what they have achieved in the past.

Companies and organizations whose leaders are within this type or group of people normally end up in pits. Example: there is a certain country in Europe by name England. This country was the inventor of the eleven-member football team, which is being used worldwide.

Unfortunately, instead of this country doing what would make it to be regarded as the best or one of the best football nations in the world; it is rather boasting itself of being the inventor of football, and because of that, none of its national football teams from the junior levels to the senior has been able to emerged as one of the giants in the world of football.

Again, there is a certain country in Africa by name Ghana. Within this country, there is also a certain football club called Kotoko. Decades ago, both the country and the club dominated African football; hence, they won a lot of trophies. Unfortunately, today, instead of them doing what it takes to win trophies in Africa, they rather boast themselves of what they have achieved in the past and because of that, they have now become participants in modern African football competitions.

Again, there is a certain political party in Ghana called CPP. This party with its able Leadership led by Dr. Kwame Nkromah legally fought for, independent of the country and won it as well; hence, it ruled the country for some years and did much marvelous and tremendous work which is still being served as the backbone of the country.

Unfortunately, today, instead of this party realizing that the method of wining an election in the country has changed, they rather boast themselves of what they had done for the country in the past with the notion that such boasting could win them election; and because of that, this party always pools less than two percent of the total votes cast of the national elections.

Detractors: the detractors are people who want things to be done as it were in the past. They always prefer the old systems, methods and ways of doing things; hence, instead of submitting, planning and responding positively to change, they rather oppose it.

Companies and organizations whose leaders are within this type of people, also end up in pits. Example: there are certain football clubs in Europe. Decades ago, these clubs were football giants in Europe.

However, instead of responding positively to the changes in football in order to maintain their positions in the world of football, they still consider football as a game of fun; hence, they criticize those who see it as a business; and because of that, some of them have been relegated to the lower divisions without being able to bounce back: and those who are still in the senior divisions are not making imparts in modern club football. And one of these clubs is Nottingham Forest.

Again, there is a watch producing company in the Western world by name Swiss watch. Years ago, this company was the world leading producer of watches; then, a small group of people within the company teamed up and produced a new watch; an electronic one for the company.

However, instead of the leaders of the company, embracing the new electronic watch, they preferred their old motorized watch to the new electronic one. Then, this new electronic watch was introduced to the other watch producing companies. They quickly accepted it, embraced it, and produced it in brands. This new electronic watch became more popular in the watch market than the motorized watch; and this caused the company to lose its popularity and leadership in the watch market. For this reason, never joke with change.

Change in the field of knowledge

However, in the field of knowledge, the Bible says in Daniel 12:4 that, in the last days, knowledge shall increase.

In fact, knowledge has increased in these days and it will continue to increase; hence, in these days of advanced knowledge, it is difficult for a person to succeed in a genuine manner without knowledge irrespective of the abilities, potentials, talents and the gifts.

Note this, the Bible says, "He that entereth not by the door into the sheepfold, but climbeth up some other way, the same is a thief and a robber". (John 10:1)

As the end result of a thief or a robber is imprisonment, death, disgrace, and above all eternal doom, so is a person who enters the success arena through dubious and all kings of evil means. It is written, "As the partridge sitteth on eggs; and hatcheth them not; so is he that getteth riches, and not by right, shall leave them in the midst of his days, and at his end shall be a fool". (Jeremiah 17:11) Therefore, never enter the success zone through foul means.

Knowledge brings success and development in life, society and a nation as a whole. It is written, "And by knowledge shall the chambers be filled with all precious and pleasant riches". (Proverbs 24:4) For this reason, upgrade yourself in knowledge in order to succeed, and to maintain your job, position, business, organization, etc.

In these days of advanced knowledge, managers, directors, and all kinds of employees of companies, institutions or organizations with lower qualifications can only maintain their positions by upgrading themselves else they will lose them in no time to those with the requisite knowledge.

Therefore, in this age of advanced knowledge, do not oppose it, but rather; upgrade yourself, especially in the field of your profession or abilities and it will be well with you. The upgrading can be through seminar, distance, formal, informal, or self education.

Entrepreneurs, leaders of companies, organizations, nations and tribes: individuals, business men and women, employers and employees, there is a time for everything; so whether you like it or not, change will take place; and it holds the key to success as well as failure.

One's success or failure depends largely on his or her response to change: therefore, foresee it, smell it, sense it, understand it, plan and respond positively to it, and it will be well with you.

Chapter four
THE SECRET OF AFRICA'S UNDERDEVELOPMENT AND THE WAY OUT TO GREATNESS

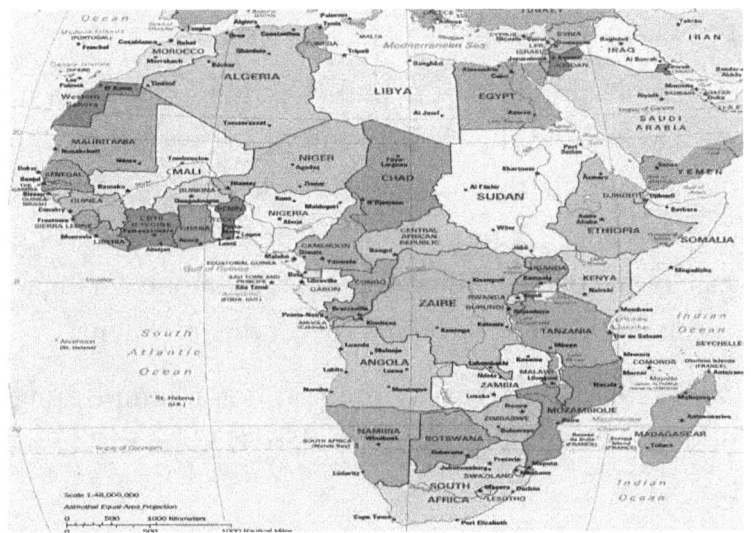

Africa

O Africa, the land of Ham, the throne of gems, the morning star of the daughters of the earth, why are you underdeveloped? Were you not also created in the image and likeness of God, with potentials and creative abilities to create, invent, manufacture, etc., why are you still underdeveloped? O Africa, and lands of Ham beyond the shores of Africa, how long will you sleep, how long will you be dependent, how long will you walk in the footsteps of Ham your father: Arise, turn away from his footsteps and climb the development ladder; for your destiny is in your own hands.

The earth is divided into seven land masses known as continents. These are: Europe, Asia, Africa, North America, South America, Australia and Antarctica. Out of these, with the exception of Antarctica due to its cold temperature, all the rest is inhabited.

However, among the inhabited continents, Africa is the second largest and the most beautiful with suitable climatic conditions. Beside the suitable climatic conditions, Africa is endowed with all kinds of natural resources such as gold, oil, gas, coal, cocoa, uranium, timber, diamond, manganese, etc., yet it is still far behind in terms of development.

O citizens of Africa, why are you not accomplishing the purpose for which you were placed by God on this beautiful continent?

When God created the earth, he made a beautiful garden popularly known as the Garden of Eden: full of trees on a portion of it, and put the man–Adam whom he created in it to dress it. It is written, "And the LORG God planted a garden eastward in Eden; and there he put the man whom he formed to dress it and to keep it". (Genesis 2:8, 15)

God put Adam in the garden to dress and to prune the trees in order to yield more fruits for the benefit of all the creatures.

However, as God put Adam in the garden to make it conducive and productive for the benefit of all the creatures, so he has divided the earth into land masses known as continents among mankind to dress and to prune the trees within them in order to be conducive and productive for the benefit of all.

Unfortunately, horns of Africa, instead of dressing and pruning the trees on the continent in order to yield more fruits for the benefit of all as ordained by God, they are rather felling them for their own parochial-interest. To be precise, instead of authorities of Africa, making use of the resources on the continent for the benefit of all as ordained by God, they are rather using them to their own advantage.

O citizens of Africa, how long will you walk in the footsteps of Ham – your father, until when will you desist from his character and embark on development?

Noah, the just and the perfect man before God in his generation, the man who found grace in the sight of God in the days of the flood, gave birth to three sons – Shem, Ham and Japheth, through whom the earth was replenished with both the white and the black race. It is written, "And the sons of Noah, that went forth of the ark were Shem, Ham, and Japheth: these are the three sons of Noah: and of them was the earth Over- spread". (Genesis 9:18-19)

However, after the flood, Noah planted a vineyard, and drank the wine thereof and was drunk. When he was drunk, he became naked; and Ham, his second son saw his nakedness. It is written, "And Noah began to be a husbandman, and he planted a vineyard: and he drank of the wine, and was drunk; and he was uncovered within his tent. And Ham, the father of Canaan, saw the nakedness of his father, and told his two brethren without (outside).

And Shem and Japheth took a garment, and laid it upon their shoulders, and went backward, and covered the nakedness of their father; and their faces were backward, and they saw not their father's nakedness". (Genesis 9:20-23)

In fact, the above scripture does not show that Ham intentionally viewed his father's nakedness: therefore, it might be an accident. But, Ham, having seen his father's nakedness, he never felt for him; hence, he didn't do anything to save him from his condition of nakedness, shamefulness and suffering but rather went out to spread the news.

However, Shem and Japheth, the first and last sons of Noah, having heard the news from Ham their brother, deeply felt for their father; hence, they went to deliver him from his shamefulness and suffering by covering his nakedness. Ham did not even bother to join his brothers to save their father from his unfavorable condition.

The attitude of Ham toward Noah, his father, indicates that he was a man without love and compassion; but that of Shem and Japheth, his brethren, indicates that they were men of love and compassion. These attitudes of Shem, Ham, and Japheth, are common among their descendants.

The Biblical accounts of their descendants are recorded in Genesis 10:1-32. But due to genealogy, migration and changes in names, to know exactly the descendants of Shem,

Japheth and the rest of Ham on the other continents, please, do a research. Thank you.

Ham's character of uncompassionate, unloving and callousness, is common among his descendants especially those in African. And these attitudes of the descendants of Ham of African towards each other or themselves, are the main cause of Africa's underdevelopment.

Love of money, love of power, shoddy work, selfish-interest, self-seeking, bribery and corruption, pull him down syndrome, fraud, black market, discrimination, sorcery, spell, envy, greed, headstrong, sabotage, jealousy, lies and the like which are by-products of unloving and uncompassionate, are common in Africa, and because of that, it is not able to develop.

O Africa, until when will you walk in your father's character: look, due to your attitude of selfish-interest, self-serving and interest in immediate sugar than tomorrow's milk and honey, you have become like Esau.

Africa has become like Esau

As Esau sold his birthright to Jacob because of food, so has Africa also sold her right and glory to the shemites and the Japhethes because of selfish-interest.

There are two types of rights in the Bible. These are: birthright and divine right. The divine right has to do with anyone whom God chooses out of brethren to accomplish his purpose, and the birthright has to do with a first born son being entitled to double portion of the properties of his father. It is written, "If a man has two wives, one beloved, and the other hated, and they have born him children, both the beloved and the hated; and if the firstborn son be hers that was hated:

Then it shall be, when he maketh his sons to inherit that which he hath, that he may not make the son of the beloved firstborn before the son of the hated, which is indeed the firstborn: But he shall acknowledge the son of the hated for the firstborn, by giving him a double portion of all that he hath: for he is the beginning of his strength; the right of the firstborn is his". (Deuteronomy 21:15-17)

But with regard to kingship, the kings of Israel were chosen by God himself; hence, it was not based on birthright but rather, on divine right.

Example: Reuben, the firstborn of Jacob, slept with his father's wife and because of that, the birthright was taken away from him and it was given to Joseph as the firstborn of Rachael Jacob's second wife; hence, Joseph received a double portion of the land of Israel-Manasseh and Ephraim but the divine right was given to Judah. (Genesis 49:8-10)

Again, out of the eight sons of Jesse, the divine right was given to David the lastborn. (1 Samuel 16:4-13)

Now, Isaac, the second son of Abraham; to whom also the divine right was given out of the eight sons of Abraham, gave birth to two sons namely, Esau - Edom and Jacob are also known as Israel.

However, God, being a God of fairness and justice, shared the rights for them. The divine right was given to Jacob and the birthright was given to Esau.

God shared the rights to them right from their mother's womb, even before they were born. It is written "And Isaac entreated the LORD for his wife, because she was barren: and the LORD was entreated of him, and Rebekah his wife conceived.

And the children struggled together within her; and she said, if it be so, why am I thus? And she went to inquire of the LORD. And the LORD said unto her, two nations are in thy womb, and two manner of people shall be separated from thy bowel; and the one people shall be stronger than the other people; and the elder shall serve the younger.

And when her days to be delivered were fulfilled, behold, there were twins in her womb. And the first came out red, all over like an haily garment; and they called his name Esau. And after that came his brother, and his hand took hold on Esau's heel; and his name was called Jacob." (Genesis 25:21-26)

In fact, the above scripture shows clearly how greedy Jacob was as well as how spirit human beings are. The struggle of Esau and Jacob, a fetus who did not know anything in the human sense, yet were able to struggle over

Rights, clearly shows that indeed human beings are spirit. Note, whoever receives the divine right automatically becomes greater than the one who receives the birthright. Therefore, even if Jacob did not receive the blessing of the firstborn son from Isaac, their father, he would still be greater than Esau because of the divine right.

But because Jacob was greedy, he wanted to have the birthright in addition to his divine right; therefore, when the time for Rebekah to be delivered was up, Jacob tried as much as possible to pull Esau back by holding his heel in order to overtake him to enjoy the birthright in addition to his divine right.

But because it was God himself who gave the birthright to Esau, Jacob couldn't achieve his aim. And because of what he did against Esau his brother in the womb, God's anger was kindled against him. It is written "The LORD hath also a controversy with Judah, and will punish Jacob according to his ways; according to his doings will he recompense him. He took his brother by the heel in the womb."(Hosea 12:2-3).

Jacob couldn't overtake Esau in the womb to have access to the right of the firstborn son or the birthright in addition to his divine right, yet when they were born, he still wanted to have it; so therefore, he was seeking for an opportunity to snatch it. Then, one day, Jacob prepared a meal, and in the course of it, Esau returned from the field (he was a hunter.)

When he returned home, he was hungry; hence, he asked Jacob, to give him some of his food; and this served as an opportunity for Jacob to achieve his aim: therefore, he made Esau to understand that, before his request for food would be granted, unless he sells the birthright to him by oath; and Esau did it.

It is written, "And Jacob sod pottage: and Esau came from the field, and he was faint: and Esau said to Jacob, Feed me, I pray thee, with that same red pottage; for I am faint:

And Jacob said, sell me this day thy birthright. And Esau said, behold, I am at the point to die: and what profit shall this birthright do to me? And Jacob said, swear to me this day; and he sware unto him: and he sold his birthright unto Jacob.

Then Jacob gave Esau bread and pottage of lentils; and he did eat and drink." (Genesis 25:29-34)

Because of food, Esau sold his birthright to Jacob by oath without considering its implication; and because of that, he lost the blessings of the firstborn son to Jacob. (Genesis 27: 1-33)

In fact, as Esau sold his birthright to Jacob because of food, so has Africa also sold its right and glory to the children of Shem and Japheth because of selfish-interest. Despite that Africa is endowed with all kinds of natural resources, the majority of the African countries are not in control of the mineral aspect of their own natural resources such as gold, oil, coal, uranium, etc.

Due to selfish-interest, self-seeking and self-serving, heads of Africa have vested the minerals in the hands of the children of Shem and Japheth, and they are controlling them; hence, the blessings of the minerals which are supposed to be enjoyed by the Africans, almost eighty-five percent of them are enjoyed by the children of Shem and Japheth; and because of that, the majority of the African countries is indirectly under the control of the Shemites and the Japhethes even though they have had independence. Oh Africa, what a pity.

Nevertheless, Africa, your own attitude has pushed you far behind as far as development is concerned, yet it is not over.

It is not over

Africa, even though, nothing was said to Ham-your father, when Noah was blessing his children: (Genesis 9: 24 – 27) and that might be one of the reasons why you have not been able to desist from his character to embark on development despite the abundance of the natural resources you possess, yet your success is not over.

When Esau sold his birthright, he lost the blessing of the firstborn son to Jacob, yet he wanted to have a blessing from Isaac his father; hence, he asked his father to bless him; but unfortunately, when his father opened his mouth, all the words which came out were negative, (Genesis 27:34-40) yet with determination, Esau was able to make it in life. (Genesis 33:9)

So therefore, Africa, as Esau was able to become successful despite the negative pronouncement of Isaac his father, so will you also be prosperous if only you will change your mind. For it is written, "Be ye transformed by the renewing of your mind". (Roman12:2)

The mind is the determinant of a person's outcome in life. Wherever direction the mind is channeled to: so shall the result be. If the mind is channeled along positive paths, development takes place and vice versa.

Note, the fact that almost all the inventions, innovations, and man-made equipment in the world were made by the Shemites and the Japhethes, does not mean they were created differently with different brain; no. We were all fearfully, wonderfully and specially made by God in his own image and likeness to have dominion over the earth. (Genesis 1:26-27)

God is full of wisdom and so has he made all human beings. Therefore, either white or black, all of us possess the creative abilities of God to create, invent, change, transform, etc.

The only difference between the developed and the underdeveloped, the rich and the poor, is the mindset. So Africa, change your mindset, channel it along positive paths, and you will be transformed.

Fortunately on your behalf, all the equipment needed for development, the Shemites, especially the Japhethes have already produced them: hence, your development has become easier; therefore, change your mindset from things which do not bring development, such as fraud, bribery and corruption, black market, indiscipline, selfish-interest, envy, high-handed, lawlessness and the like and put on compassion, equity, justice, truth, mercy, discipline, patriotism as were exhibited by their excellencies Dr. Kwame Nkromah and Nelson Mandela, and above all, love, and you will make it.

Where there is love; discrimination, sorcery, bribery and corruption, envy, selective-justice, selfishness, sabotage, callous, unsympathetic, jealous, lies, perversion, bias and the like which cripple development is scarce. Love does not seek its own, but rather the interest of all; and this brings peace, unity and development.

Tribalism and Tribal sentiments in many African countries whereby some tribes despise or see themselves as more important than others, which do not bring peace, unity and development can only be erased by love.

Love brings people together as one man with one soul, one mind and one spirit, irrespective of their racial, cultural, financial, educational, religious, tribal, social and political backgrounds; and this makes impossibility possible. It is written, "Behold, the people are one and there is nothing that they cannot do". (Genesis 11: 1 -3)

Love is the source of development. All the countries which have developed are countries whose citizens are patriotic.

Due to love or patriotism, there is a keen competition between the advanced countries; each of them wants to become the best in the world scientifically, technologically and economically; and because of that, things which do not bring development, such as a black - market, lies, pull him down syndrome, jealousy, fraud, selfishness, lawlessness, bribery and corruption and the like are rare or uncommon in those countries.

It is love or patriotism that enables the citizens of the advanced countries consider the interest of their nations first by exempting themselves from shoddy works for the sake of development, it is love that enables the leaders and citizens of the advanced countries consider the welfare of future generations of their countries, it is love that enables the leaders and citizens of the advanced countries consider the development of their countries than their own pockets, it was love that drove the leaders of the advanced countries to come out with the good policies which have yielded them development.

Citizens of African countries, you are not inferior to the citizens of the advanced countries; you were also created in the image and likeness of God with the same creative abilities and potentials of the citizens of the advanced countries to transform the world economically, technologically and scientifically; therefore, change your mindset, fear God, put on patriotism, love and compassion, and you who are seen today as beggars; will be seen as lenders in no time.

About the Author

Daniel Nana Kwame Opare is a citizen of the family of God, the body of Christ. He is a philosopher, Bible scholar, an ardent and a prolific writer. He is divinely ordained to reveal the mysteries in the word of God for revival and transformation of individuals, the church and the world as a whole.

His books are highly written for spiritual, physical, mental and material transformations of lives.

Some of his books are: What every believer must know, Enlightenment and Success garden.

www.ingramcontent.com/pod-product-compliance
Lightning Source LLC
Chambersburg PA
CBHW072114290426
44110CB00014B/1910